SACRED STORY

Living Your Story

10 BIBLICAL PRINCIPLES THAT MATTER

BY COURTNEY GARRETT
AND LAURA WILCOX

Introduction

What matters as you live your God-authored story? Relationships. Freedom. Obedience. Transformation. Surrender. Identity. Contentment. Purpose. Forgiveness. Endurance. Courtney Garrett and Laura Wilcox created the *Living Your Story* study to encourage every woman that her daily decision to follow God matters. Each topic contains relevant Scripture along with questions to explore Biblical principles and concludes with an inspiring story from the Sacred Story collection. This study guides a woman no matter where she is in her faith journey toward insight and growth about how the Word of God relates to living her story. It can be worked through individually, one-on-one, or within a group. For those who are prompted to facilitate a small group, the leaders guide at the end of the material offers practical steps and suggestions.

About the Authors

Courtney Garrett received her Masters in Christian Education from Dallas Theological Seminary. She served as the Director of Women's Discipleship at her home church, Grace Bible Church, in Houston, Texas, for six years and is a regular contributor at Sacred Story Ministries. She is the author of *101: Exploring the Basics of the Christian Faith.* For over 15 years, Courtney has taught and encouraged women in the truth of God's Word as she lives out her passion of equipping women to disciple the next generation. Courtney is married and loves being the mom of two boys.

Laura Wilcox received her Master in Biblical Studies from Dallas Theological Seminary. Laura launched Sacred Story Ministries (www.sacredstoryministries.org) to come alongside women as they discover and live their God-authored stories in light of His Word. Her background includes serving for over two decades with an international mission organization and publishing the study *Capture My Heart, Lord.* Laura is passionate about women finding restoration and redemption in their own stories while also investing in the lives of others for the sake of Christ. Laura resides in Houston, TX and loves travel, a good book, and time with friends.

1

Relationships Matter

SACRED STORY

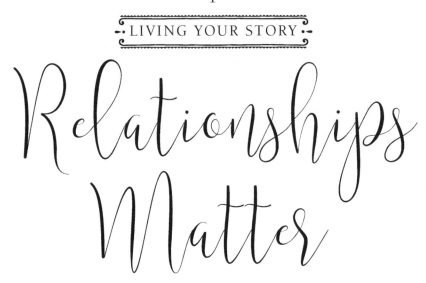

LIVING YOUR STORY

Relationships Matter

Relationships form the core of our stories. The chapters of our lives begin with family relationships and expand to include friends, teachers, boyfriends, doctors, roommates, coworkers, neighbors, and many others. We kick off our time together by looking at the significance of relationships in our stories.

Why do relationships make such a powerful impact in our lives?

Our parents help form the way we think about ourselves, others, and life in general. Give an example of how your mother or father shaped your thinking.

Relating to people can result in many experiences we need for growth. We learn what compassion looks like, how to communicate our needs, how to develop friendships, and what it means to love. On the other hand, relating to people may damage our ability to grow as a person.

What are ways relationships make a negative impact on us?

From the beginning of time, God created human beings to live in relationship with Him and others. God's designed relationships to always be life-giving and promote growth. The Bible, claiming divine inspiration, says, "And God created man in His own image, in the image of God He created him; male and female" (Genesis 1:27).

Do you see people relating to others in ways which show what God is like? If so, how?

Upon creating the first human beings, Adam and Eve, God walked with them in the garden and they experienced God's presence at all times. In Genesis 1:29, God says to them, "Be fruitful and multiply, and fill the earth and subdue it. . ." and then the Bible concludes, "God saw all that He made, and behold, it was very good" (1:31). Tragically God's design for relationships didn't remain in a state of "very good." God's protection of Adam and Eve included the mandate, "From any tree of the garden you may eat freely; but from the tree of the knowledge of good and evil you shall not eat, for in the day that you eat from it, you shall surely die" (Genesis 2:16-17).

Why do you think God prohibited Adam and Eve from eating from this tree?

We don't know definitively why God put the tree in the garden. We do know that God wants to be trusted. We also know that true love is love that is given when a person has a choice.

The serpent, bent on disrupting the harmony in the garden, approaches Eve and tells her God is lying about the consequences of eating from the tree: "You surely shall not die! For God knows that in the day you eat from it your eyes will be opened, and you will be like God, knowing good and evil" (Genesis 3:5). When Eve decides to believe the serpent over God, she eats from the fruit and offers it to Adam. This action of choosing to go their own way instead of God's way means sin enters the human race. The immediate effect is spiritual death and as a result, a loss of intimate friendship with God.

Read Genesis 3:6-13.

What emotions do Adam and Eve experience? How do they deal with the reality of their sin? How do we hide from God today?

The broken relationship with God through rebellion resulted in the event known as the "fall of mankind." Sin occurred and separation from God entered the human race. In the book of Hosea God pours out His heart about the broken relationship (11:5,7,8) saying, "Because they refused to return to Me. . . So My people are bent on turning from Me. . . My heart is turned over within Me. All my compassions are kindled."

Not only does God grieve the separation He experiences from those He created but also the devastation of sin within human relationships. When Adam and Eve conceived two sons, Cain and Abel, seeds of hostility grew as Cain became jealous of Abel and eventually killed his brother (Genesis 4:1-9).

What examples do you see in society of anger and jealousy tearing down relationships?

The book of Romans describes the entrance of condemnation into the human race through Adam's sin resulting in spiritual death. Romans 3:23 states, "For all have sinned and fall short of the glory of God. . ." and 6:23 explains, "For the wages of sin is death. . ." As a holy God who is perfect in His character, He cannot be in the presence of sin. A great chasm exists between God and those He created.

God longs to restore the consequences of the fall of mankind. His divine love reaches out to men and women in their spiritual state of death. He provided for the penalty of sin through the sinless life of Jesus Christ and His death on the cross as payment for sin. Romans 5:19 expands, "For as through the one man's disobedience (Adam's) the many were made sinners, even so through the obedience of the One (Jesus Christ) the many will be made righteous." *Righteous* carries the meaning of "right standing" with God.

When Jesus died on the cross for sins, He proved He had the authority to lay down His life on behalf of mankind. Three days later, Jesus was raised to life and walked out of the tomb. This miraculous event validated His victory over the death penalty for all who trust His work on the cross. Ephesians 2:8-9 explains receiving forgiveness with God based on faith in Christ: "For it is by grace you have been saved, through faith—and this is not from yourselves, it is the gift of God—not by works so no one can boast."

Why do we feel like we can earn a relationship with God through our own efforts?

Our relationship with God is restored when we come to know Him through trust in Jesus Christ. Romans 10:9 states, ". . . if you confess with your mouth Jesus as Lord, and believe in your heart that God raised Him from the dead, you shall be saved."

Have you come to a place of receiving God's love and forgiveness in Christ? If you haven't, who can you tell to help you with the next step?

If you have embraced God's love and forgiveness in Christ, share a brief summary with your group about your decision as you feel comfortable.

Relationships matter in our stories. A relationship with God through Jesus Christ represents the vital core for knowing the Author who designs the days and hours of our lives for a purpose. He is able to bring good out of the pain we experience in relationships. He also generates great blessing as we know Him better through others and continue to become more like Him in the way we love those around us.

Take a minute and read Elise's* story, "My Childhood Chaos," below. Consider how relationships with God, other people, and herself made a difference.

My parents divorced when I was six and I have no memory of them together. My mom who had been a stay-at-home mom was suddenly a single working parent. It was a very big change for a very little girl. Both of my parents remarried within a year. This was a very confusing time, full of different people entering my life. My mom remarried a very unstable, abusive man. She felt like her decision would give us stability; instead it brought more chaos.

My mom couldn't handle my sister and sent her off to live with my dad and stepmom. In the midst of the first 18 months, my stepfather sexually abused me. My memories of that time are hazy. I knew enough to know that something was very wrong with what he was doing. It made me feel very strange and uncomfortable. My mom and stepdad fought a lot. There was a lot of yelling. I think he left a time or two and came back. No one really liked him, but my mom stayed.

I finally told my mom about the abuse a few years later. Unfortunately, her answer was to sit me down with both of them and ask me if I wanted my stepdad to leave. As a child then, and an adult now, I wished she had booted him straight out of the house. I was a timid child and couldn't turn out a grown man crying in front of me. So he stayed. And my issues and the past were swept under the rug.

During all of this chaos at my mom's house, my dad and stepmom were such solid parents. They had a happy, warm home. The contrast created more confusion about my mom's house. Why hadn't she stood up for me? Why was she still with him? Did it even happen? My yucky feelings about my memories continued for a long time.

*The author's name is a pseudonym.

I eventually told my dad and stepmom in college. It was very hard for me. No one had ever believed me. They immediately took care of me in all the ways that I had hoped someone would. It was very validating. My mom finally divorced my stepfather. And life moved on until I became a mom which brought up a lot of emotions again. It seems to me that we judge our parents as confused children, young adults, and parents one day.

I was a new Christian when I went through those feelings again as a parent. I talked with my mom, asking some very hard questions. She asked for my forgiveness. I even called my stepfather hoping for validation, but he wouldn't confirm anything. I went to therapy and worked through a lot of confusing emotions. I went to church where I learned so much. All of those things helped me move forward and heal.

These are my thoughts as I reflect on what happened: I am tremendously grateful for such a good example in my dad and stepmom. I needed a model of stability and love. I would remind another woman who has been violated of the importance of telling someone what happened. It is horrible to feel alone, weird, and sad. We all need to be heard and validated. Words are powerful and when I said them out loud, it released something inside of me.

I can't change what happened to me, but I can change how I react. We can help each other by sharing our experiences. I grow a little every time I hear someone's story. My faith has been tremendous in healing my heart. I didn't have Christ in my life when these things happened to me, but God had a plan for me. He is a parent who will NEVER let me down! He is good and bigger than all of the sin in this world. Some bad things happened to me as a child, but there is real HOPE in Christ. He stands before me and I'm new. There is more than this broken world we live in and I'm so grateful for that!

"I can do all things through Christ who strengthens me" (Philippians 4:13).

For Reflection:

How did Elise experience the positive and negative impact of relationships?

How does her faith change her perspective on the harm she suffered?

2

Freedom Matters

SACRED STORY

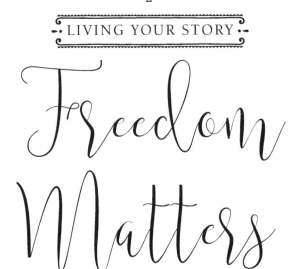

Freedom Matters

Freedom is defined as, "Liberation from slavery or restraint or the power of another." The chapters of our stories include finding freedom from sinful patterns, wrong thinking, and destructive habits. It may be worry, addiction, bitterness, guilt, unhealthy dependency on another person or a host of other possibilities. In this session we reflect upon experiencing release from those things which entangle us.

When have you witnessed worry, addiction, bitterness, or unhealthy relationships become a prison in someone's life?

A typical human response to being trapped is to bargain with God for release. In Paul's letter to the church at Galatia, he warns believers to avoid the trap of trying to please God by doing "good" or performing religious acts. **Write out Galatians 5:1 below.**

Jesus came to set us free. When we try to gain freedom in our strength Paul says we are living in the flesh. By doing so we spin our wheels without the Lord's supernatural resources. The apostle Paul describes the struggle between the flesh and the Spirit in verses 5:16-18. **Read these verses and summarize the battle we face.**

Believers win the battle between the desires of the flesh and the desires of the Spirit by depending on the power of the Holy Spirit. Paul calls this walking in the Spirit and explains the contrast between living in the flesh and the Spirit. Read verses 5:19-21 and 5:22-23 and together write the fifteen acts of the flesh on the column on the left and then list the nine fruit of the Spirit on the right.

Acts of the Flesh   **Fruit of the Spirit**

As you look at the two columns, what stands out to you?

The Spirit produces the fruit of Jesus' life and character as we "keep in step" with Him each day. Read Galatians 2:20 and 5:24 which explain a believer's oneness with the crucifixion of Jesus.

What does it mean to be crucified with Christ?

How does a believer's union with Christ make a difference when confronted with self-centered living and/or sin?

Read Ephesians 4:30-32. We grieve the Holy Spirit when we live in bondage to sin. Think about a destructive habit, attitude, relational dynamic, or other entanglement in your story.

How can "counting it crucified with Christ" by faith enable you to live in the Holy Spirit's victory?

Read Ephesians 5:18-21. What command is given concerning the Holy Spirit? And what are the results?

Filling of the Holy Spirit in a believer's life occurs when he or she yields to His control. Just as faith is required to receive Christ for salvation, faith is also the vehicle for experiencing the filling of the Spirit.

What does it mean to receive the filling of the Holy Spirit by faith?

How is the Holy Spirit working in you through the challenges in your story?

Freedom matters in our stories. The good news of the Gospel releases a new experience of freedom from those things which entangle us because a relationship with Jesus Christ means we possess the Holy Spirit within us. By acknowledging His presence and depending on His power, we move from a place of defeat to a place of victory.

Read Laurie's story "From Insanity to Serenity" describing her courageous journey to find God's freedom in her story.

> Hi, my name is Laurie, and I'm an alcoholic. That is how I represent myself at Alcoholics Anonymous (AA) meetings. I've learned alcoholism is a disease. It is hereditary. My father's mother and my mother's father were both alcoholics. Both my parents were alcoholics who drank at home. To the outside world my family looked

like something off "Leave It to Beaver" or "The Donna Reed Show." This disease affects your mind, body and spirit. I have also learned alcoholism is a symptom of the real problem.

Women can cross that imaginary line from being a "normal" drinker to an alcoholic quickly. That was the case for me. I had all the traits of a garden-variety alcoholic. I always drank to excess in my young adult years. However, when I got married and had my children I only drank socially.

Once I hit my forties, I started drinking more than socially. One thing led to another and I found myself not able to control my drinking. I didn't lose my family, job, house, car, etc. I lost my sanity. All I did was think about what time I got off work, when I could get that next drink, "when, when, when." I stopped going to functions away from my house, because I knew better than to drink and drive; especially since I had had two serious car accidents in my late teens due to drinking and driving.

As an isolated drinker, I had become "just like my mother." The one thing I didn't want. My mother died at 49 from a brain hemorrhage, having passed out while drinking at home. I was only 23 when she died. I didn't want my kids to feel the pain I had felt. After a few years of swearing I'd quit, trying every possible way to stop, I finally broke down and reached out for help.

I called AA. I will always remember the kind young woman I spoke with named Kristy. Her encouragement and helpful information led me to my first meeting on September 4, 2008.

AA is spiritual program. You are asked to believe in a power greater than yourself. Belief in this power will relieve you of your alcoholism. Some folk who have a problem turning their will and their life over to God start out by turning it over to the group first. My higher power is GOD.

I attended church on a fairly regular basis throughout my life. I saw everyone having faith in God and I was always envious. I just had no idea how to have a relationship with God through Jesus Christ. I had never read the bible and didn't know how to carry on a conversation with folks who seemed to know God. I felt stupid and embarrassed. AA taught me how to do all those things; even more so, how to talk to God Himself. I also learned a lot about growing my relationship with Him from people in my church.

Once I turned this over to God, my life became more manageable. I lost the desire to drink. My sobriety date is September 5, 2008. My problems became easier to handle. I used to think in order to pray, you had to say all the "thee's, thou's, etc." I now know I can talk to God, just as simply as I am writing these words. When my day becomes crazy I "let go, and let God" take care of things. I just need to wake up each day and let Him lead me. When I try to be in control, my life gets out of whack. When I let God be in control, I have a calm serene day. I live happy, joyous and free thanks to finding my faith. When I first took steps toward freedom from addiction my faith was but a "tiny mustard seed." Now I have a total mustard forest! I am confident God will be there to guide me through anything life brings me.

For Reflection:

What shifts in Laurie's thinking allowed her to find freedom?

How can you "let go, and let God" be in control this week?

3

Obedience Matters

SACRED STORY

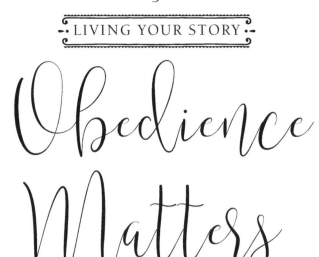

Obedience Matters

From the time we are young we learn the difference between right and wrong. Parents show us what it means to abide by rules and why it is important to obey. Sometimes it is a matter of our safety and protection. Other times it is teaching us the proper way to relate with others. In this session, we will look at why obedience in our stories is more than a list of rules to follow.

What are your first memories of learning the difference between right and wrong? What were the consequences you faced which helped enforce the rules?

Growing up, did your temperament tend toward more of a "rule-follower" naturally or did you have more of a rebellious nature?

Read Exodus 20:1-17. Like our parents, God has a list of "rules" or laws in the Bible He wants us to follow.

In your opinion, how are God's rules or laws different than the rules from growing up?

List the first four commandments which relate to God.

List the next six commandments which relate to others.

If you are child of God and have accepted Jesus as your Savior, there is peace found in knowing we cannot earn salvation through abiding by a list of rules. We are saved by grace alone, through faith alone in Christ alone (Ephesians 2:8-9). There is nothing we can do to earn love, acceptance, or even blessings from God; however, the Lord does desire obedience in His children.

What is our motivation for obeying God if we don't have to earn our way to heaven?

Read the story of Abraham and Isaac in Genesis 22:1-18. Isaac was the long-awaited child for whom Sarah and Abraham had prayed. He was the first-born son of the chosen people God had promised.

What did God call Abraham to do?

How would Sarah have felt watching her husband and teenage son walking way?

Our trust is often tested when obedience to God goes against our logic, desires, and emotions. Like in the life of Job, God doesn't always explain Himself in times of testing. We are often called to believe in His goodness and perfect sovereignty, even painfully surrendering what we think we want most of all.

What enabled Abraham to trust God and obey Him in this situation?

How did God provide?

In verse 14 Abraham declares God as His provider.

How has God's past provision in your story increased your faith? Describe a specific example.

We often forget the many ways the Lord answers prayer. Consider journaling as a tool to recall God's faithfulness for yourself as well as for the purpose of passing on to others.

What can we learn about obedience from Abraham and Isaac's story?

While difficult to see some times, obeying God always results in blessing. While the blessing may look different than expected, we never lose when we follow God's will and commands.

Read Deuteronomy 28:1-13 and list all the blessings God promised Israel if they chose obedience.

Obedience is hard sometimes especially when the world says the opposite of what we read in Scripture. It is counter-cultural to remain sexually pure before marriage, forgive a friend who has hurt you deeply or give thanks to God in even the hardest of situations. Think back over the different chapters of your life.

What are some examples in your own life of obeying God and the blessings that resulted?

What have been the consequences you have faced when you've chosen disobedience?

What tempts us to go against God's Word and His plan?

Obedience matters in our stories. Tim Keller a pastor of a large church in New York City explains the good news of the Gospel: we are more sinful and flawed in ourselves than we ever dared believe, yet at the very same time we are more loved and accepted than we ever dared hope. In ourselves we are sinful and rebellious and want our own way BUT God's desire for a life of obedience is grounded and covered in His unconditional love for us. Not because He is a harsh taskmaster who but a loving Father who wants to give us His very best and show us again and again that following Him is the way to true life.

Read Stacy's* story *When God Called Me to Stay* and think about how obedience affected her life and those around her.

> How often do we pray for God to change our situation? We land somewhere outside of our comfort zone and pray that God will take away our pain and that He will lead us down a better path. For me, it was 1986; I had been out of college for just under two years and was working in the technical recruiting industry in the Dallas area. The company that I was working for was expanding and I was offered a promotion to move to the Houston office. They had a Houston team in place but told me that there were a "few issues in the Houston office."
>
> Immediately after arriving in Houston I began to see how difficult this situation was going to be. The first issue was that Houston was suffering very high unemployment of over 9 %. This was of course more than a small problem in the recruiting business. My biggest struggle though was not the unemployment rate but the other employees in our Houston office. Not only were none Christians, they also ridiculed me for my faith. The other managers in Houston told me I stuck out like a sore thumb. My supervisor in Houston would come in to my office and write that our new name was going to be called the "Christian Staffing Center" and laugh.
>
> This was an unbearable situation and I started to pray for God to show me the open door to a new situation. But the more I prayed the more God told me to stay. I couldn't believe it; I really thought that I needed to remove myself from this job. It was not only the team and the teasing but more importantly my immediate boss was pushing me constantly to do things I felt were unethical. Truly a situation where I could have felt justified walking out of, but I really wanted God's direction and He was saying to stay.

God's message to me at that time was one simple message; He was calling me to stay. The message from Philippians 4:6-7 was what I felt God was telling me. "Do not be anxious about anything … And the peace of God which transcends all understanding, will guard your hearts and your minds in Christ Jesus." I felt he was calling me to be a Christian in business and he wanted me to live my faith 7 days a week-not just on Sunday's. If I would do that for Him then I felt that God was promising me His peace. My fiancé and I (now my husband) discussed this and prayed. My words prayed for "God's will in my life" but I know my heart prayed for change and for God to call me to a new situation. Yet, when He called me to stay-I obeyed.

That first year in Houston was so difficult, I struggled with fears that I would be fired for taking the stands that I took and also my own personal desire to quit. However, in small ways whenever I needed encouragement, God was there with me encouraging me and offering his perfect peace. I would see Him in the workplace. Sometimes it was in a coworker asking for advice, or other managers thanking me for taking the tough stands that I took. Even in my immediate manager that so ridiculed me when I came to Houston, I started seeing small signs of God's work in her life.

God ended up keeping me there for over 20 years, our Houston office was slowly transformed. My boss became my friend and my sister in Christ. The change in our Houston organization was nothing short of miraculous. It was so amazing to see God's hand at work. God's lesson has stayed with me through my adult life; He has showed me that although my situation may not be easy, when I seek His will, I will have His peace. With God's peace all things are possible.

For Reflection:

How did Stacy work through her desires vs. what she felt like God wanted her to do?

*The author's name is a pseudonym.

How does her story encourage you to obey the Lord?

Transformation Matters

Transformation Matters

One thing in life remains certain: we always face change as a part of our stories. Changes occur in ourselves and others through evolving circumstances, interactions, and emotions. In this session, we reflect on being transformed on the inside as the chapters of our stories unfold with the unexpected.

What kind of uncertainty are you currently experiencing in your story?

Let's begin by looking at an example from Scripture of women who faced uncertainty. As background, a woman named Naomi and her husband Elimelech live among God's people in the land of Judah. They encounter a severe famine and as a result of the lack of food, they relocate with their two sons to the land of Moab where idols are worshiped. During their ten-year stay, Elimelech dies and then both of Naomi's sons marry Moabite women. Sadly, her two sons die also. At this point, Naomi decides to return to Judah because she hears the famine ended; her daughters-in-law, Ruth and Orpah, volunteer to accompany her. This is where we pick up the narrative in Ruth 1:6-22. Read the passage and consider the following.

How does Naomi counsel her daughters-in-law Ruth and Orpah to deal with the unexpected loss (vs.11-12)?

How does Naomi interpret her circumstances (vs. 13, 20-21)?

Ruth and Naomi found themselves in the midst of both external and internal change. External change represented by the loss of their husbands and thus, the source of security in ancient culture. Internal transformation for Ruth takes the form of how to respond to Naomi's plea to return to Moab and Naomi faces the challenge of how to think about God while processing so much loss.

How do Ruth and Orpah respond to Naomi's counsel?

Read verses 15-18. What does Ruth's response to Naomi reveal?

Difficult circumstances in the form of loss in these women's stories result in grief, compounded by the struggle with how to walk through the unknown.

What emotions have you experienced during a time of insecurity?

What does our tendency to resist the unknown show us about our hearts?

Unwelcome circumstances create space to know God more deeply. Our responses cultivate or close the space to know God better.

What are some ways to cultivate our relationship with God?

Unexpected situations present an opportunity to grow personally and spiritually. Through meditating on Scripture, prayer, and seeking out support and resources we can be transformed. On the flip side, just like Ruth and Naomi's culture offered a solution, the "world system" which the Bible says is under the control of the evil one tempts us to follow its solution when faced with insecurity. Read I John 2:15-17.

How can a time of uncertainty become a breeding ground for "the lust of the eyes, the lust of the flesh, and the boastful pride of life?"

Our spiritual enemy wants to tempt us to panic and seek for a solution outside of God's guidance. We can resist the temptation to do so by affirming the Lord's power to lead and provide. Read 2 Corinthians 3:17-18. In this chapter, Paul explains how the transformed lives of those in Corinth are evidence of God's truth in Christ.

As a reminder from our session about freedom, who is the Holy Spirit (vs. 17)?

How does He guide us?

Why does cooperation with the Holy Spirit transform a believer's life (vs. 18)?

Changing circumstances in our story offer the opportunity to become more Christ-like.

How can you have a Spirit led approach to uncertainty in your current story?

When something shifts in a woman's story, her response can also affect other people positively or negatively. Reading the entire book of Ruth is a treasure to be stored up when you are able. For our purposes, compare Naomi's words in 1:20-21 to what God accomplished for her and Ruth in 4:13-17.

How did those around her see God's hand?

How does your response to uncertainty affect the people around you?

Transformation matters in our stories. Because change is a constant theme, we can learn to respond to uncertainty in faith instead of react out of insecurity and pride. By clinging to the Lord and trusting His hand upon our circumstances we will find Him faithful every time. God uses the changes we encounter to mold our character and influence those around us.

As you read Joye's story "Finding My Security," reflect upon her response to change in her life.

My husband, Don, and I met and married in San Diego, CA in 1971. After our wedding, we moved to his small hometown of Borger in the Texas Panhandle so that he could join his Dad in the road construction business. We lived lifestyles that reflected the world like partying, drinking, not attending church. I spent my days as an elementary teacher.

Two years into our marriage the thirteen year old daughter of some dear friends of ours died when a car hit her on her bicycle. We grieved with the family at this tragic loss, but did not know how to comfort them. We were amazed as we witnessed their faith. They were committed Christians and immediately clung to the truth that they knew their daughter was in heaven and that they would see her again someday. This "Good News" they talked of was new news to Don and me, so out of curiosity, we decided to visit their church. After the first Sunday, we were intrigued by what the pastor was teaching from the book of Romans and continued to attend each Sunday. Three months later the Holy Spirit had softened our hearts and both Don and I prayed to receive Christ as our Savior.

I had looked for love in a lot of wrong places through my teenage and young adult life. I came to realize that the love relationship I wanted and needed was Jesus! A peace settled deep into my heart as the Holy Spirit came into my life and I rejoiced in the firm promise of heaven someday. Soon Don and I were blessed with two boys, Bryan and Timothy, three years apart, and ultimately we adopted our babysitter, Dena, at the age of 18 who was being raised by her elderly grand-parents. We became very active in a small Bible-centered church where we studied and diligently applied God's Word to our lives. I ultimately developed a women's ministry and Don joined the elder board. God had captured our hearts and we offered all of our lives to be used by Him.

In 1987, I marked Ps 73:25-26 in my Bible: Whom have I in heaven but You? And besides You, I desire nothing on earth. My flesh and my heart may fail, but God is the strength of my heart and my portion forever. (NASB) Through those words, God impressed upon me that I could not be certain of anything or anyone on earth. My security needed to be in Him and Him alone. That truth motivated me to study the Bible more deeply and allowed it to transform my mind. I became convinced that God loves me, He is good, and He is sovereignly in control of all that happens in life.

Those truths burrowed deep into my mind and heart and prepared me for March 29, 1989. After eighteen years of marriage, I received news that my beloved husband had died instantly in a car accident. In the midst of my shock and disbelief, my mind was flooded with the truths I had earlier learned: God is good, He loves me, and there are no "accidents" with Him. As I chose to embrace these truths and accept my Heavenly Father's will, the Holy Spirit ministered to my hurting, wounded heart, much as Jesus was comforted in the Garden as He reluctantly, yet willingly, yielded to His Father's plan (Lk 22:41-43).

Two days after Don's death, I read Ps 27:13-14: I would have despaired unless I had believed that I would see the goodness of the Lord in the land of the living. Wait for the Lord; be strong and let your heart take course; yes, wait for the Lord. Those words encouraged me to trust deeply in God. He faithfully provided for me and my children during that painful, difficult time through unexpected financial provision, support of family and friends, and strength to face each new day without a father and husband in the family. God proved even more how much He loved me and cared for my every need as I continued to trust in His goodness.

More than two decades later I thank God that all of my children are committed Christians and that I have the unexpected privilege to serve on the faculty at Dallas Theological Seminary. God has transformed my pain and loss into an amazing opportunity to share His love and truth to those training for Christian ministry. I remain confident in God's abiding presence which allows me to enjoy an inner peace as I wait expectantly for the unfolding of His perfect will in the years ahead.

For Reflection:

How did Joye allow her loss to transform her? How did her decision affect others?

What are examples of the solutions the world offers to deal with uncertainty?

5

Surrender Matters

SACRED STORY

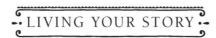

Surrender calls to mind a great battle scene where one army advances against another. At some point, it becomes evident to the weaker army that they will indeed be overtaken and defeated. They fly the white flag of surrender attempting to salvage the remainder of their troop and their own lives. Surrender implies a "giving up" or "giving in" after a struggle. In this session we will explore the necessity of relinquishing the authorship of our story.

What comes to mind when you think about the word *surrender*?

Read 1 John 1:8-2:2.

What must we recognize about ourselves before we can truly surrender to the cross?

What comfort do you find in these verses?

When we understand that we are desperate sinners, we see our brokenness, depravity and utter dependence on Him for life. C.S. Lewis said, "Fallen man is not simply an imperfect creature who needs improvement; he is a rebel who must lay down his arms."

How does sin make us all rebellious towards God?

Read Luke 7:36-50. What did the woman have to surrender in order to come to Jesus?

What stands out to you about how she interacted with Him?

How did her loving act demonstrate what she believed about Him?

How did the Pharisees view her and what she did for Jesus?

We cannot surrender to Jesus without true humility. Humility requires us to take a proper view of ourselves as sinners and understand we are nothing without Him. Jesus' greatest demonstration of humility came when he subjected Himself to the Cross and all the suffering that went with it. All for us! Read Psalm 51:17.

Contrast the attitudes of the woman who anointed Jesus and the Pharisees.

Do you believe in God's ultimate authority over all of your life? For instance, His will for where you live and work, your marital status, whether or not you have children or even the number of children He might give you, etc.

What are some areas that you hold on to, even subconsciously, where you would rather call the shots?

What are your fears about submitting those areas to the Lord?

The truth is, we were never made to rule our lives. Believing that God's ways are better results in peace and ultimately joy.

What does Isaiah 55:8-9 remind us about His perfect will?

How do the following verses encourage you?

John 10:10

Ephesians 3:20-21

Surrender matters in our stories. When we come to terms with our tendency to make our stories about us, we can give over our understanding of how things ought to go. We find a place of peace by believing God's character and living for His glory in every chapter.

Read Jennifer's moving story "My Desire Became Consuming," and consider her journey of surrender.

> My husband and I went through three years of infertility before our twin boys were born. Before they turned a year, we started infertility treatments because we both strongly wanted more children. After two pregnancies resulting in miscarriages, we decided to stop the treatments for a while and give my body and heart time to heal.
>
> Then seven months later I became pregnant again. It was a shock to both of us! We found out on Mother's Day, which was such a gift from the Lord. But at my seventeen-week appointment, we found out that our baby had died just a few days before. I can't begin to describe my heartache. Samuel David was delivered on Aug. 10th, 2011.

I can't really remember the days after his funeral. But my God, my God…He enveloped us with His peace. I remember one morning as I lay in bed, I didn't want to do anything and I prayed to the Lord and asked Him to help me. In a gentle whisper I heard, Stand, all you need to do is stand. So I did. I needed to stand physically and spiritually in His truth. He loves me, He has never left me, He is for me and He is good.

Six months after losing Samuel, I became unexpectedly pregnant again and miscarried around five weeks. Then five months later I had an ectopic pregnancy and miscarried. I soon went to the crazy place. Why was this happening? Haven't I been through enough pain? What is it that God wants me to learn? I just want another baby…why is this so hard? Doubt and lies from the evil one penetrated my heart. I felt unreachable by God and so alone.

I saw a reproductive endocrinologist who ran test after test and basically told me that my eggs were old and there weren't many left. It was possible I could become pregnant again but it could take years.

I felt the walls of my heart going up and kept God at an arm's length because He was responsible for my pain. I started walking in offense. God had offended me. I wanted to protect my heart from the One who caused the pain. Even though He had been the One who created these miracle babies, I was too focused on what He hadn't done for me.

I started looking on the internet for how to increase pregnancy in your late 30s and how to decrease your chance of miscarriages. I wanted to be in control. In December, my husband lovingly told me that my desire to have more children had become an idol. He asked if I had surrendered this to the Lord and I said yes. He then said he didn't see any peace in me regarding this. I didn't know how to respond. We prayed about it and I knew it wasn't surrendered.

A week or so later I was talking to a dear friend who told me how the Lord asked her to tangibly surrender a desire she had. I felt the Lord asking me to do the same thing. Shortly after, my husband and I had the day together. I told him that I wanted to visit the cemetery where Samuel was buried. I grabbed a sticky note and wrote Georgia Ann… my baby girl name.

Looking at Samuel's headstone, I knelt down. I knew God was asking me to place the sticky note on Samuel's headstone, completely surrendering my baby girl and any other babies. It was one of the hardest things I've ever done because in my mind I thought if I truly give this over, and He chooses not to give us any more children…will my Jesus be enough? The answer was yes. I then let go of that sticky note. But it wasn't just a sticky note…it was my heart, my dreams, my babies. They were all His now.

I didn't want to get up. My husband just held me as I cried and cried. But eventually we did get up and a peace came over me like none other. I finally felt free from the bondage of the very thing I wanted so badly. I had turned my desire into an idol, making me captive to it. Psalm 118:5 says, "In my anguish I cried to the LORD, and he answered by setting me free." I'm now walking in freedom and fully know that my Jesus is enough.

For Reflection:

What process did Jennifer go through to arrive at peace about surrendering her desire?

No matter what you want God to do for you, how can you draw strength from Jennifer's journey?

As an update, Jennifer and her husband welcomed Georgia Ann Lacey into their family on November 1, 2013 through the adoption process. They are praising God for all that He has done!

6

Identity Matters

SACRED
STORY

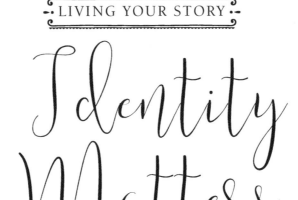

Identity Matters

Suzanne is a pastor's wife who serves the Lord faithfully. When her son showed signs of learning and relational challenges, she and her husband spent years seeking experts to discern how best to meet his needs. One of the difficult aspects of his behavior was a tendency to throw tantrums past the toddler stage. During one taxing season when it seemed like no answers were in sight, she recalls her six-year-old son acting out at the grocery store and eyes were on her as if people were saying, "Get your child under control. . .He must need more discipline. . ." Suzanne struggled with placing her worth in how her child was behaving, allowing the situation to determine how she felt about herself. When she reminded herself of God's view of who she is as His daughter, Suzanne was able to remain proactive in parenting without letting it define her.

The word identity is defined as "the fact of being who or what a person or thing is." **What titles or roles tend to make up a woman's identity?**

How we think about who we are makes up the foundation of the chapters of our stories. When we embrace Jesus Christ as our Lord, the essence of who we are changes, bringing forth a new identity. This identity is unshakeable because of our union with Christ. **Write out 1 Corinthians 6:17.**

When a person unites with the Lord through faith, spiritual benefits and characteristics are present which didn't exist prior to knowing Him. **Read I Peter 2:9-10 and write out a description of the believer's new identity.**

The descriptors in I Peter of who we are in Christ are powerful truths which affect how we think, act, and relate. **Look up the following verses and complete the statements below about the effect our identity has on us.**

John 15:16 I did not choose Christ but He ...

Hebrews 4:14-16 Because I belong to Jesus who is my high priest I can ...

Titus 2:13-14 Jesus gave Himself to redeem me from all wickedness and to purify ...

Ephesians 5:8-10 Being united with Jesus means I am commanded to live as ...

Ephesians 5:18-20 My union with Christ includes surrendering to the filling of the Holy Spirit who moves me to ...

Which of the five truths above is most meaningful to you right now? Why?

Being united with Jesus Christ doesn't mean we become a better version of ourselves. It means we belong to a spiritual family with new DNA which provides the ability to become the people God designed us to be. While our temperaments, personalities, and talents are unchanged, our motivation and expression of who we are is vastly different because of whose we are. **Read Ephesians 4:17-24 and summarize in your own words what it means to live out your new identity in Christ.**

In the fourth chapter of Ephesians Paul is referring to the Gentiles as the general population who have not come to a saving faith in Jesus Christ. **How does Paul describe the Gentiles' spiritual state and mindset in verses 17-18?**

What are their resulting actions and attitudes in verse 19?

In verses 20-21 Paul shifts his focus to believers in Jesus. What does Paul remind the Ephesians about the difference in who they are?

What is the description of the old self and the new self in verses 22-24?

What are the three actions listed in these verses when it comes to relating to the old self and the new self?

To help us get a handle on how the "old self" and "new self" operate, consider the following examples. A woman's "old self" may base her worth on how she looks or how well she performs at a particular task; whereas God says the truth about her "new self" is that He declares her lovable and acceptable in His eyes apart from outward appearance or performance. A woman's "old self" may not feel comfortable expressing her needs or feeling like her needs are valid; yet God says the truth about her "new self" is that she is a member of a spiritual family who is united to each other and as a result, she can lean on others. A woman's "old self" may slant the truth to make herself or a situation look better; in contrast God says that He is honored when her "new self" practices honesty and accurate communication in line with her identity as His child.

What are other areas that the old self might be at work in a person's life?

What does it look like to put off the old self and put on the new self in these areas?

Take a few minutes for personal reflection. Ask God to show you an area where you struggle to put on your new self in Christ or tend to live out the old self. Write a prayer asking for His strength and praising Him for the privilege of being conformed to the image of Jesus Christ.

Identity matters in our stories. Becoming One with Jesus Christ through faith means we are called a new essence where God transforms us into the women He created us to be. When we begin to grasp the reality of whose we are and the spiritual truths which accompany our new position and relationship, we are changed. As you and I make choices to assume our new identity, the chapters of our stories are packed with purpose and power to be Christ-like.

Bunmi is a woman who found herself caught in a performance trap. Realizing her identity is not defined by her achievements, Bunmi found the courage to trust God's path. Soak in her story below.

Exhausted by the grind of my second year as a general surgery resident, I tried to energize myself by recalling my big dreams. I planned to enter a fellowship program to further specialize, become an academic surgeon with built-in research time, and take sabbaticals where I would work in impoverished regions in Africa while training other doctors.

In the present moment though I felt miserable. I thought the demands on my time would be short-lived but instead I realized my career path required more of my focus. I gave myself a pep talk- life will return to normalcy next year when I begin my first of the two research years involved in my academic track. I looked forward to a saner pace of life with no more 80+ hour work weeks.

Fast forward to my third year when I received a prestigious grant including the opportunity to work with two mentors, a stellar researcher and a pediatric surgeon. I reached the next step to realizing my dream, but why did I feel even more miserable? I lived under a cloud with my motivation at an all-time low. The need to perform and pretend I wanted this goal became harder. By the fall, I called a dear friend confessing suicidal thoughts and my need for her support to throw out the rest of the pills my dentist prescribed after surgery.

I found myself disillusioned and depressed. I didn't know how to keep going. That's where God met me. I couldn't be picky about how I experienced Him—death and despair stood on one side and a cry for help on the other. I encountered the reality of His Presence in new ways. The first came when a group of friends prayed for me at the end of a conference. I sensed something changed but I couldn't put my finger on what. The following week, I realized I no longer lived under a perpetual cloud. I still identified certain thoughts as stemming from fear, despair and shame, but my desire to die as the solution vanished.

As the oldest child in a culture which values achievement, telling my parents I no longer desired to be a surgeon proved to be the hardest thing. They threw me the equivalent of a wedding reception when I graduated from medical school, complete with formal invitations, cakes, custom dresses, an acapella choir and a DJ! As much as I enjoyed them being proud of my achievements they were not living my life. And I had to face reality: I didn't like my current life or its prospects. One evening during the Christmas holidays, the words just came out: "I'm planning on leaving my residency." My declaration hit my family like a torpedo and things remained uncomfortable for a very long time.

I returned to my research obligations after the holidays. I felt led to dial down socially as the Lord spoke to me through Song of Songs in the Old Testament, focusing my attention on the crux of everything. I couldn't let go of surgery until I knew deep down God created me for love and defined me by love. By relying on my credentials for my worth, I often turned to my accomplishment as a surgeon to battle insecurities as a single woman and a woman of color. During this time God taught to me to rest as His beloved daughter, releasing the need to perform.

The next hurdle of telling my program director loomed before me. I wrestled with how to do so. A resident leaving a program normally could result in a logistical nightmare because of the rotations. But God went ahead of me and amazed me by the way He orchestrated things. It turned out that in order to balance the number of residents in the research and clinical programs, they needed one less resident.

The number problem provided the perfect opening for a conversation with my program director. He responded with such encouragement, even voicing questions about whether his current role suited him. Some people didn't understand why I made the choice to leave, expressing their concerns. Somehow God gave me the strength to let go of the need to live for others' expectations and move forward to discover where passion, joy and His purposes met.

I am learning to live from my heart, to trust my Heavenly Father in the way He designed me to live. I feel a new and growing freedom to explore with Him. I've been surprised by the things I love to do as a writer, makeup artist, and budding fashion designer – and all by His grace!

For Reflection:

What were the results of Bunmi placing her identity in her achievements and other peoples' expectations?

What decisions did she make which helped bring her out of despair?

Like Bunmi, how can finding rest in being God's beloved daughter change your outlook?

7

Contentment Matters

SACRED STORY

Contentment Matters

In the book *Calm My Anxious Heart* by Linda Dillow, there is a quote from a missionary named Ella Spees who served with her husband in Africa for over 50 years. She faced all types of hardship during those years but was able to maintain a right perspective despite the challenges. Ms. Spees had a prescription for contentment that was summed up as follows:

*Never allow yourself to complain about anything—not even the weather.
*Never picture yourself in any other circumstances or someplace else.
*Never compare your lot with another's.
*Never allow yourself to wish this or that had been otherwise.
*Never dwell on tomorrow—remember that tomorrow is God's, not ours

This is certainly humbling to read, isn't it? It is very easy to complain about a lot of things on a regular basis. How do we arrive at a place where we have this attitude of contentment regardless of our circumstances?

Where are you struggling to find contentment in your story right now?

The *Holman Bible Dictionary* defines contentment as an "internal satisfaction which does not demand changes in external circumstances." We often believe that changes in our circumstances will bring about a more fulfilling life; however, the discomfort that comes with the challenges we face cause us to need the Lord.

Read Philippians 4:19. What does this verse promise?

Why is it possible to be content even in difficulty?

The reality is we are often confused about our "needs" and our "wants." If God promises He will meet every need, why are we still dissatisfied? It is easy to fall into a trap of greed or entitlement. We feel we deserve this or that (we don't) or we must have certain things (not true). This doesn't mean we can't grieve over unmet expectations. It also doesn't mean contentment is the same thing as apathy. Contentment calls us to surrender outcomes to the Lord as we pursue goals and express our desires, trusting His plans are good no matter what circumstances we encounter.

Read Philippians 4:11-13. What does the author, Paul, say about the circumstances he has faced?

What do you think is the secret he is speaking of in v. 12?

It is a secret because it is not immediately apparent and it is the antithesis of all the visible things the world offers. Elisabeth Elliot, missionary and author, said, "The secret is Christ in me, not me in a different set of circumstances." Her point is well taken. Picturing life differently will never bring about contentment. Christ is the answer. Paul learned this reality as he often endured persecution, death threats, hunger and other serious situations. If Paul found contentment in his circumstances, surely can't we?

One of the pitfalls that leads to discontentment is comparison. Read Matthew 20:1-16 and answer the following questions.

According to v. 3 what was promised to the laborers?

What caused the early workers to resent their pay?

What role does "fairness" play in this situation?

Can you think of a recent situation when you feel that God didn't act "fairly?" How did you feel?

This parable rubs us the wrong way at first glance. The frustration of the early workers is understandable; however, it was only when they heard what the other workers were paid that they became upset. They compared and that's when they got angry.

According to verse 15, what motivated the owner to pay like he did?

Life can be hard and unfair; however, the Bible tells us that in Christ, we lack nothing. Psalm 34:10b says, "…Those who seek the Lord lack no good thing." What if we woke up every day and said, "Lord, whatever you have given me today is sufficient. I lack nothing because of you."? Paul mirrored this attitude. Everything he had in Christ was more than enough for him to be content.

What keeps you from feeling you have everything you need?

How is the restlessness we often feel a tool the Lord uses to focus on Him?

Think back over the first question and where you are struggling at the present to find contentment. Read Lamentations 3:22-24. What hope do these verses offer you in the middle of your situation?

Contentment matters in our stories. We can seek the Lord and ask Him to be our portion daily especially in those times when we are restless and needing to see that His grace is sufficient for all things. He shows us, ultimately, it is Him—His Word, His presence, His perspective—that bring fulfillment and purpose. Praying for the Lord to change something in our lives isn't wrong but clinging to that change as our hope for happiness will never lead to contentment. Sometimes there are circumstances in our lives where we will have to fight to find a degree of contentment (e.g. a difficult work environment, a challenging marriage, a prolonged period of infertility, a continued journey of singleness). It's at these times where we cry out to the Lord and ask for His hope, His perspective and a renewed sense of purpose.

As you read Mary's story below think about how her perspective of the Lord changed her ability to walk in contentment.

Most people find it hard to believe that 10 years ago, I was in a wheelchair, barely able to lift my arm to feed myself or brush my teeth. Today, I'm living a healthy, normal life, working full-time, enjoying endless possibilities.

But back then, I was in constant, debilitating pain. My arms felt like my raw nerves were tearing away from their sockets. I had a continual sharp pain in my lower back. When I moved my neck, or even my eyes, I experienced pain that lasted for weeks. Every movement felt like I injured myself and couldn't heal. Finally, I could barely move.

What made matters worse was that this all started just after I moved to Budapest, Hungary as a missionary. My decline was so rapid that I got to this disabled state only three months after I first arrived, and initial medical testing yielded no diagnosis. No one knew what was causing this. After several months I was diagnosed with fibromyalgia, for which there is no definite treatment plan.

Thus began a horrible roller coaster journey that lasted over a decade. I continued to live in Hungary for six years with my health going up and down. I travelled back to the States occasionally, seeking treatments that might help, and at times I would find some improvement.

Finally, in 2003, my health plummeted to an all-time low and I moved back to California permanently. Through a process of trying many, many alternative medicine approaches, I gradually discovered the combination of treatments that have worked extremely well for me. People from all over the world began contacting me to find out what I did to improve, so finally I wrote a book about my story that mentors people with chronic illness in how to find their own unique plan for improvement. It's called Break Free: Journey with God through Chronic Illness to Health.

One of the most difficult parts of this experience was in my relationship with God. I found it difficult to understand how God could be good, loving, and kind and at the same time allow such horrible pain to the daughter he loved. If I saw my daughter struggling with so much pain, and I had the power to stop it, I would do so immediately. Why wouldn't he?

I remember one particularly difficult day, after many years of pain, when I got fed up with God and told him so. I was alone in my house and I let him know exactly how mad I was about this whole situation. I even told him I was not going to speak to him anymore! I held out for about three days, but finally crumbled because I needed him so desperately. I said, "I'm sorry Lord for this temper tantrum, but I'm extremely frustrated and distressed." God immediately spoke to me in my spirit, saying, "Mary, you are like a person who is banging her head against the wall over and over in trying to understand this. You can keep on banging your head, letting it get bruised and injured, or you can simply accept that there are things you will not understand this side of heaven. My ways are not your ways."

I realized that I could either accept the paradox that God is good, loving, kind, and he allows very bad things, or continue to wrestle with this in frustration and despair. Irish missionary Amy Carmichael struggled with her own long-term illness until she came to a place she called "contentment with the unexplained." This is the place that I finally reached. It is a place of resting in the integrity of God's character, even though he allows very bad things.

Through this health crisis, I grew deeper and richer in so many ways. I can identify with James when he said, "... you know that the testing of your faith develops perseverance. Perseverance must finish its work so that you may be mature and complete, not lacking anything." (James 1:4)

For Reflection:

What struggle did Mary have about the character of God?

How did she come to a place of contentment?

Ask God to give you "contentment with the unexplained" this week.

8

Purpose Matters

SACRED STORY

"Being successful and fulfilling your life's purpose are not at all the same thing; You can reach all your personal goals, become a raving success by the world's standard and still miss your purpose in this life." This quote by Rick Warren, author of the *Purpose Driven Life*, reminds us that we are designed to live with purpose and not simply success. The world's says success is measured by wealth, relationship status, appearance, talent, and other markers. In contrast, God desires to weave eternal purposes into each chapter He writes in our story.

Who or what comes to mind when you think about living with purpose?

What are some barriers to a person finding a life of purpose?

Read Ephesians 2:1-2, 8-10. Paul reminds the Ephesians of the gift they have received. **How is a person rescued or saved from being dead in his or her sins?**

What role did your efforts or good works play in the salvation God gives to you through Jesus?

When you and I place our faith in Christ's work on the cross we receive the right to become children of God. (John 1:12) **How does Ephesians 2:10 describe a believer in Christ?**

The words "masterpiece, handiwork, and workmanship" are used to describe a believer in Christ. Merriam-Webster defines masterpiece as "a work done with extraordinary skill; especially: a supreme intellectual or artistic achievement" and handiwork is defined as "work done by the hands, work done personally." The word in Greek is *poeima* where we derive our English word poem. **Combine insight from the definitions and the Greek meaning to write out a sentence below of how God views believers.**

Our lives point to the One who is the Author of our stories. What does it mean to you personally that you are God's masterpiece?

God's purposes for His children include becoming the person He created each to be. Because He exists outside of time, He already sees believers as completely formed in Christ. Yet the believer's experience on this earth is a process of knowing Jesus better and becoming more like Him, often referred to as sanctification. **Write key words and phrases from these Scriptures which explain God's purpose of making believers Christ-like.**

Romans 8:28-29

Philippians 1:6

Galatians 4:19, 5:22-23

The Holy Spirit sanctifies us as we depend on Him. He changes our thoughts, motivations, desires, behaviors, and attitudes. **Far from exhaustive name the areas below which reveal the character of Christ being formed in a believer.**

Galatians 2:10

I Corinthians 6:18-20

Colossians 4:3, I Thessalonians 5:16-18

I John 3:16-18, Galatians 6:9-10

God works purposely through your life as your story unfolds with blessing, challenge, and heartache. **How have you come to know Him better?**

What qualities do you see Him producing in your life?

What does Ephesians 2:10 say about God's part and a believer's part in good works?

God does care about a person's good works and yet not to secure his or her place in heaven. It is quite the opposite since faith is the only way to receive His gift of eternal life. God designed you to carry out good works as His workmanship when you place your faith in Christ. He set them in motion before you knew Him so that you can live out a life of purpose. It's mind boggling to think about but nevertheless Scripture says it's true!

Write out the following verses describing the divine role God calls believers to fulfill in the space provided.

Matthew 28:18- 20

I Corinthians 3:7-9

II Corinthians 5:18-20

In most instances God doesn't take us straight to heaven when we come to faith in Christ. He leaves you and me on earth to participate in His purposes of building the kingdom. The three verses above among other Scripture describe the spiritual mission entrusted to all believers of sharing the good news of Jesus Christ and discipling believers. This mission is often referred to as the Great Commission.

Think about those who imparted truth to you about Christ and living for Him. How did their faithfulness make a difference in your story?

The highest privilege we have as we "pass through" this life is to invest in the stories of people, so they can know Jesus and the hope of His calling. **What are obstacles you face to sharing the message of Jesus Christ's love and forgiveness and discipling those who come to know Him?**

What is a step(s) you can take to overcome obstacles to participating in Jesus' mission?

Purpose matters in our stories. As you depend on the Lord through your chapters, you become more like Him. You can be confident that God never wastes your experiences, positive and negative, because He uses them to increase your faith and benefit others. When you take steps in the power of the Holy Spirit to join His mission of sharing the good news and discipling believers you experience supernatural joy and fulfillment. Just like receiving Christ as Savior is an act of faith enabled by God's grace, God also pours out His grace so you can live your story for His purposes.

April's story is a beautiful example of how our Lord continues to seek and save the lost. Be encouraged today as you think about how God uses imperfect people to reach others for His kingdom and grow them into maturity in Christ.

I was raised in a religious home. We went to church, but I spent most of the time counting the organ pipes at the front, anxiously waiting for the service to end. I have no real memory of reading the bible at home or talking about Jesus. I was baptized, took my first communion and was confirmed. Honestly, it all meant nothing to me.

I lived my life as a "good girl." I made good choices to please my parents with no thought of pleasing God. I would not say I lived in a strict home, but it was just easy to be good and hang around the good kids. After graduating from high school, I went to college where I joined a sorority and met a lot of new friends. A lot of Christian friends!

Looking back my Christian friends invited me to do things, but I had no interest. I went to church maybe once in college to selfishly pray for a good grade in one of my classes. I discovered alcohol and began to socially drink, at times a little too much. Drinking made it easy to talk and to let loose and have a little more fun than the "good girl." I saw the Christians around me and thought their wholesome lives were boring; however, I noticed a certain peace and joy they had, that I did not. What I didn't know is that they were praying for me.

I would jump into relationships to fill the void. The highs of the attention, affection, and physical intimacy I experienced in a new relationship amounted to fleeting happiness. I experienced deep pain when they ended and there was no real joy in my life. After college I moved back home and got a job. I went out drinking with friends on Friday and Saturday and I went to church on Sunday morning, but still felt lonely. I continued to drink and date and after a few failed long-term relationships, I was exhausted. I could not get out of my own way for so many empty years. My Christian friend who I knew in college invited me to join a Bible study at her home.

This study turned out to be a huge turning point in my life. It introduced me to the fundamentals of Christianity which humbled me and opened my heart to a new life with Jesus at the center. I found a woman who was farther along in her faith to show me how to depend upon Christ. I became comfortable in my singleness for a while. My old ways of looking to the highs of social drinking and relationships no longer brought me happiness. I cried out to God to break me out of my cycle.

I stopped reading "self-help" books to bring me out of my pit and started reading the Bible—God's Word. I desired Christ centered relationships that would grow me in my relationship with him. I felt God transforming my heart. Before, I was living a life where I was at the center and committing "respectable sins." On the outside I looked like I had it all together, but inside I was a mess. With God's help over time I was able to stand against the temptation to make dating relationships my obsession.

Today, I do my best to live a surrendered life of purity through the strength of Jesus Christ living in me. I remain so grateful to have met and married a man whom I share faith in Christ as a foundation. We have walked through some mud along the way, because God never promises an easy life as Christians. God blessed us with our children and we pray that they come to know Christ at an early age as we also pray for Him to be the center of our home. I cling to Philippian 4:8 as a specific prayer for God to work in us as a family: "Finally, brothers and sisters, whatever is true, whatever is noble, whatever is right, whatever is pure, whatever is lovely, whatever is admirable—if anything is excellent or praiseworthy—think about such things."

I feel more convinced than ever in my Christian beliefs which causes me to be more intentional in my conversations and friendships. I pray that God will bring somebody to me who I can pour my faith into and share His truths which have transformed me. When I struggle with being misunderstood or rejected on occasion because of my decisions and behaviors of the past, I remember that I no longer place my hope in people and circumstances to bring me peace and joy. I find strength to forgive myself through putting my faith in God's complete forgiveness described in His Word. Psalm 103:11-12 says, "For as high as the heavens are above the earth, so great is his love for those who fear him; as far as the east is from the west, so far has he removed our transgressions from us."

For Reflection:

In what ways did the Christians in April's life impact her?

How did April find purpose when she came to know Jesus in a personal way?

LIVING YOUR STORY

Forgiveness Matters

SACRED STORY

Forgiveness Matters

Corrie ten Boom was a Danish Christian woman who lived in The Netherlands during the second World War. She was burdened for the persecution of the Jewish people which led her and her family to hide many men, women, and children so they would avoid being taken away to death camps. Her sacrificial act led to her imprisonment in a concentration camp where she remained for almost a year. Miraculously, and due to a clerical error, Corrie was released and spent the remainder of her life teaching people about God's love and forgiveness. At one point during her public speaking engagements, she came face to face with a man who had been one of her cruel guardians at the concentration camp. He had become a Christian and wanted to ask for her forgiveness for the awful things he had done. She extended forgiveness only because the Lord gave her the ability to do so. She became famous for this act of forgiveness as she continued to teach many people that forgiveness must be a mark of every Christian.

When is the last time you had to forgive someone for something, whether the offense was big or small?

The unique distinctive that sets Christianity apart from other belief systems is forgiveness. Christianity hinges on the greatest act of forgiveness the world has ever known, the sacrificial death of Jesus on the cross. He simultaneously paid for our sins and forgave the penalty we deserved when He willingly died for us. As Christians, our call is to emulate our Savior by extending forgiveness to those in our story who have wronged us.

The issue of forgiveness needs to be revisited again and again. We can easily forget how difficult it is to truly forgive until we are facing an emotionally charged situation. We can try to move on by sweeping it under the rug; however, Scripture calls us to forgive—even commands it. Doing the real work of forgiving another person requires the supernatural power of the Holy Spirit in the heart of a willing believer **in Christ.**

Read Ephesians 4:32 and Colossians 3:12-13. What do these verses say about forgiveness?

What is the motivation for forgiving one another according to these verses?

How can this motivation move us to forgive others?

Until we grasp the significance of our own need for forgiveness in Christ, we will never be able to engage in truly forgiving others. Our sin was so great and such a tremendous offense against a Holy God, the only remedy was a radical solution—a perfect sacrifice, God's own Son. Once we see that we have been forgiven so much, we will grasp why God commands us to forgive also.

Read Matthew 18:21-35. List the observations you see in these verses.

Based on the notes in the ESV Study Bible, a talent was a monetary unit worth about twenty years of wages. The obvious point of the servant owing ten thousand talents (v.24) is to demonstrate the impossibility of the servant ever being able to repay his master. Contrasted with the debt his fellow servant owed him, a hundred denarii (denarius being a day's wage), we see the great discrepancy.

How does this parable shed light on God's grace in our lives?

How can this help us when we are in a situation where forgiving another person is very difficult?

Forgiveness is never easy but it becomes possible when we have the right Gospel-oriented perspective.

The word forgiveness is based on an accounting term which means to cancel a debt. As we relate to other people in our lives, we too must make the choice to cancel the debts, real or perceived, others commit. Forgiveness is not: blowing off an offense, excusing the other person's behavior, letting go or forgetting the situation, being silent or letting enough time pass that you "get over it." Most importantly, forgiveness is also not determined by our feelings.

When have you had difficulty laying aside your feelings to forgive someone?

What motivated you to extend forgiveness to that person?

God commands that we forgive—it's for our own good. Unforgiveness can lie like a sleeping giant in our heart.

Read 1 John 2:11. What happens when we choose to hold a grudge and withhold forgiveness from someone?

The Lord wants to set us free from the bondage that occurs when we choose to withhold forgiveness. Whether we realize it or not, when we are wronged by another, that person makes our mental short list of offenders. You may not even know you have a mental list but the reality is most of us do. People make your list because of hurtful words, actions or behaviors against you. Pain is also caused by something another didn't say or do.

Think about this idea of having a list in your mind of those who have offended you. Does anyone come to mind that you feel you need to forgive? Take out a separate piece of paper and write down any names that come to mind.

Forgiving another person is essentially a secret transaction between you and the Lord. It really doesn't have much to do with the other person; although we often feel our forgiveness is contingent upon the other person saying this or that. Here are five helpful steps in seeking forgiveness through prayer.

1. Acknowledge the hurt to the Lord.
2. Tell the Lord how it made you feel (i.e. properly grieve the situation).
3. Express to the Lord your decision to cancel the debt. Surrender your right to justice.
4. Accept the person just as they are. Extend forgiveness even if the other person does not demonstrate change you feel is warranted.
5. Be willing to risk being hurt again.

True freedom is found in forgiveness. It may take days, weeks or months to work through your mental list through prayer. Keep in mind that you can truly forgive someone but still be reminded of the person and offense. When those thoughts come to mind, choose to recall the decision you made to release the person and ask the Lord to help you find peace again. The Lord may lead you to seek reconciliation with a person through a conversation; however, reconciliation may not be possible and forgiveness is not dependent on making peace with the person through a personal conversation.*

Read Psalm 32:1-2. Why is this person call "blessed" in these verses?

Do you sense the blessing of forgiveness in your life these verses speak about? Why or why not?

Forgiveness matters in the chapters of our stories. The process of forgiving is difficult; yet it also comes with great blessing when we choose to obey God's command. Looking again at the cross and what Jesus endured on our behalf gives us the motivation to walk in freedom as we extend forgiveness again and again to those who have wronged us. Let us not forget the forgiveness we need from others for all the wrongs we have committed too. Matthew 7:5 reminds us to first remove the log in our own eye before seeking to remove the speck in another's eye.

Kate's story describes her horrific childhood contrasted with God's deliverance and the beauty of forgiveness. As you read her story, think about the inability we have in our own strength to forgive.

Shaking in the cold, my three brothers and I huddled under a discarded boat waiting for hours for the click of the lock on the door and our father to let us into the house. As an eight-year-old little girl I longed to run into my Daddy's arms when he came home from work and hear him tell me he loved me at bed time. Instead, I encountered daily fear and intimidation by the man whose role as a father dealt abuse in my life. Far from the intended love, he beat my brothers and me for years with any item within reach. Cruelty described my normal as a child and I hated my father for it.

My mother had just turned 24 when she decided to leave my father who was 50 years old at the time. However, my mother's intent to distance herself from my father's grip eluded her. One year as the winter ended in northern California, she mustered up the courage to leave and we stayed with a friend in a nearby town. We hoped to remain hidden but like times past, he found us and acted out in rage by stalking us, running us off the road, slitting the tires of my mother's car, and peering into the house where we fled. We couldn't outrun our life of fear.

When spring came my mother devised another escape, explaining she wanted us to move forward as a family without my father and needed to take care of details. She took my brothers and me over the Easter break to stay with my grandparents. Having no recollection of meeting my grandparents, I remember being scared to enter their home. The only things I knew about my grandmother I heard from my father who called her a witch. My mother assured us we would be alright. Spending time with my grandparents proved to be very different from our lives at home; we enjoyed food in abundance, new clothes and shoes, and most drastically, we felt free from terror.

The time arrived to reunite with my mother. During the four-hour drive we collided with a discarded muffler on the highway causing our tire to blow out. The repair lasted a couple of hours until we continued on to our destination. Upon entering town, I recall my grandmother's sudden declaration, "Something is wrong. I feel it. We need to get out to the house." I discovered later my grandmother knew the Lord and listened to the Holy Spirit.

My grandparents dropped my brothers and me off at a friend's house and hurried out to our house of horror. The presence of a SWAT team and ambulance provided more than enough evidence to confirm my grandmother's fear. My mother had dashed out to the house to retrieve a few items of little value, but didn't realize my father laid in wait for us and she drew her last breath in pain as he murdered her. Overcome by his own fears, he killed himself.

Though I didn't know about God, I distinctly remember in my eight-year-old mind, when I heard what happened, thinking something or someone stepped in to save us with the tire blow out. Otherwise, the timing meant we would have been at the house with my mother as we always went along with her.

Many people advised my grandparents to place us in foster care saying we were damaged beyond repair. My grandmother couldn't do it and my grandfather supported her. At age eleven, I came to know Christ and decided I wanted to serve the Savior who loved me more than I ever imagined. Less than a year later I learned at camp about the power of forgiveness and released my father for the years of torment and for taking my mother. In that moment a physical weight lifted from my body like I've never felt before.

It looked like I was destined to live with hatred but God provided a way for me to be free from the pain of another person's destructive actions. To this day, the feelings of hate no longer exist. I really don't have any feelings at all toward my father; it seems like another life. What I gained from such difficult circumstances includes an immense gratitude for life, sacrifice, and compassion. God brought beauty to my soul when I chose to forgive.

For Reflection:

What do you think Kate's life would have looked like if she didn't forgive her father?

Whether an offense is grave like taking a parent from a child or less severe but nevertheless hurtful like words of slander, the five principles of forgiveness presented in this session apply. **Can you recall what those steps are?**

*Sacred Story is indebted to Laura Seifert (www.yesministries.net). Some of the material presented in this lesson is based on her teaching on this subject.

10

Endurance Matters

SACRED STORY

--- LIVING YOUR STORY ---

Endurance Matters

The book *Unbroken* tells the true story of World War II officer Louis Zamparini. His amazing feats of endurance begin when his plane is shot down over the Pacific Ocean. Attacked by sharks and shot at by the Japanese Louis stays afloat on his life raft for an unheard of 47-day period. Nearly dying of starvation and dehydration, Louis prays that God might save him. His torment at sea ends with washing up on the worst torture island the Japanese occupy. As a prisoner of war, Louis' need for endurance continues beyond what he could ever imagine.

The definition of endurance, "the ability to withstand hardship or adversity," offers a window into a significant theme in living our stories. Even if not as drastic as being held captive during war, all of us encounter situations in our lives which make us want to give up. We are not alone as God knows the impact of difficult circumstances on our hearts. He provides encouragement through His Word about the reward that accompanies endurance.

What examples have you seen of a person's ability to endure which inspire you?

Hebrews 11 applauds the faith of the men and women in the Old Testament who followed God even when they did not see the fulfillment in their lifetime of His promise to send the Messiah. **Read Hebrews 12:1-3 and think about the Christian life as a race to a finish line.**

Endurance Principle No.1
When participating in the race of faith the runner keeps in mind that others have crossed the finish line. **What phrase in verse 1 describes the "finishers"?**

How does knowing ordinary people have made it to the finish line encourage you?

Endurance Principle No. 2
When running a race it is vital to get rid of extra weights which slow down the runner or cause the person to become tangled up and trip.

How does verse 1 refer to these hindrances?

What are examples of "entanglements" in thought, attitude, and action that may become hindrances over time?

How is sin a burden the believer takes off?

Endurance Principle No. 3
The runner finishes the race by maintaining focus. A runner looks ahead to see where she is going, eventually making her way to the finish line with friends and family cheering. In the spiritual realm, a woman who engages in the race of faith looks to Jesus to guide and encourage her. She stays on course and will be rewarded at the end.

Why is it imperative to remember Jesus is the "author and perfecter of faith" (vs. 2)?

As the author and perfecter of our faith, Jesus Himself needed motivation to endure His suffering. Verse two says the "joy set before Him" gave Jesus strength to endure. **What does this mean?**

As believers, we also have been promised joy during and at the end of the faith race.

Look up the following verse references and write out the reason for the believer's joy.

Philippians 4:1

I John 1:3-4

Revelation 19:6-7

How does the joy "set before you" increase the stamina required for your faith race?

Looking to Jesus fuels our capacity to endure during hardship, suffering, and waiting.
What are practical ways you can "fix your eyes" upon Jesus?

Endurance Principle No. 4
The runner considers the One who is worthy when encountering resistance or setbacks.
While we are fixing our eyes on Jesus, what does Hebrews 12:3 say to think about?

The word hostility in this verse is explained as "unbelief and every kind of opposition." Jesus encountered an immense amount of difficulty as He sought to complete His mission. **Look up the following Scripture references and describe what Jesus endured.**

John 7:5, Mark 3:21

Luke 9:58

Luke 22:1-4

Matthew 27:27-31

What hostility or opposition do you face in running your faith race?

How does Jesus' endurance give you strength to keep going?

Philip Yancey, author and speaker, shares this perspective, "Endurance is not just the ability to bear a hard thing, but to turn it into glory." This reality became true when we follow the story which kicked off this session. Against all odds Louis Zamparini survived a very hard thing: his horror of being a prisoner of war for years. Louis eventually gave his life to Christ after being released from the camp. Jesus healed him of the anger and rage he held toward his torturers who unleashed unthinkable hostility upon him. Louis' story is a beacon of light to the world of Jesus' power to turn a very hard thing into glory.

Look up Romans 8:34. How did God turn Jesus' endurance into glory?

Jesus lives to make intercession for believers since He made a way for men and women to receive forgiveness for sins and eternal life through His death and resurrection. God calls Christ followers to sacrifice for others in bringing forward His glory. **What are examples of enduring for the sake of God's glory?**

God is not calling us to endure some circumstances in our stories. For instance, not every hostile relationship is meant to be endured. Sometimes God leads us to make a change and leave a situation. Other times He wants us to seek growth in a challenging situation by trusting Him for new patterns of thinking and relating. **How can you know the difference between Spirit led endurance and endurance that is based in faulty perceptions?**

Read Galatians 6:8-9. What is the promise in verse 9 when we do not give up?

What situations and circumstances in your story are tempting you to give up or give in to sin? How can you lean into the presence of Jesus to give you fresh endurance?

Endurance matters. Running the race of faith requires more endurance than we often think is possible. By looking to Jesus, we fuel our ability to endure hardship, waiting, and difficulty over a period of time. Our endurance is never in vain as God replaces our weariness with a harvest when we place our story in His hands.

Grace's* story is a beautiful example of finding God's strength during impossible circumstances. As you read her story, think about those areas where you are tempted to give up.

At the age of thirty, I loved my job and my friendships. But I wanted a family, and finally that happened when I married. I was wise enough to expect challenges, but never imagined the course life would take. My husband and I were soon thrilled to welcome Jacob, our baby boy into the world...truly the best gift I had ever received! I was working full-time and managed juggling career and home responsibilities. I do remember, however, thinking that I was becoming more "shallow" than I wanted to be and that I had been spared from grief in my life...but those were just passing thoughts and I kept going.

Sixteen months after Jacob was born, Shannon and Lisa were welcomed into the world with just one push each. Unlike my first pregnancy which was more natural, I loved the epidural and wanted to hug the doctor! I was so thankful to have two healthy baby girls and was also terrified at the logistics of the months ahead. How will I do this?

Shortly after the girls birth, I developed a severe headache that was unlike migraines I have dealt with previously. My mom had planned to stay with us for a month to help and the headache occurred on her birthday. She found me slumped over in the bathroom unable to move or speak. In the ER. I was diagnosed with an ischemic stroke at age 34. Months later we found out what happened … I reached up and ripped the carotid artery, dissecting it; a rare event that could happen to anybody. I was unable to receive a certain drug because of my post-partum condition. I just had to let the stroke take its course. And it took a lot.

I remember most details of the stroke as I was conscious the whole time. Initially I felt fuzzy or a bit confused, and by the end I had lost all speech. My right side was completely paralyzed and I was helpless lying in a bed in the stroke unit. It was an unbelievable event for our family and a bitter birthday memory for my mom, who ended up staying six months. The hospital stay was an intense month of PT, OT and speech therapy with breastfeeding in between. Because it was the only thing I could do for Shannon and Lisa, with the help of family and friends, and the support of my doctors, the babies were in my room during the day, although I could not lift them because of my arm...a typical feeding of the babies became quite the production!

Even when I left the hospital and started the five months of out-patient therapy, I could not say my name, my husband's name or my children's names. I went from a wheelchair to a walker to various canes to walking on my own. There were also cognitive deficits because a stroke is a brain injury. The best example I can give is the realization that I could not pack a diaper bag. Now, a lot does into packing the diaper bag for my little crew...baby diapers, toddler diapers, wipes, toys, snacks, etc. But I panicked the day I realized I could not process all of it. So I became desperate and driven to recover.

As reality sunk in, I experienced dark days. On one memorable day I was in my closet and had hobbled in there with my big leg brace on and no use of my right arm. I stumbled and became angry with God. As a Christian, I had believed in God and trusted him but was not doing well with this impossible situation, and of course began asking why. I got mad at God and thought, "I'm done with you; I'm done with praying and asking for Your help." I tried to cuss but I couldn't because my speech was so bad. It was a dark place spiritually and in every way. I left the closet resolute never to pray again, and when I almost fell within a few minutes, I found myself asking the Lord for help. That made me mad and made me cry. The Bible says He is faithful when we are faithless. How I needed his mercy then and still do today.

There was great progress in my recovery, and it was bittersweet. Because my speech was greatly affected, I found myself in a lonely place. One day, my dad who was there for support, repeatedly helped me say "house" and "horse." We both cried because it was so difficult and mentally draining and I was tired anyway from having three kids under 3 years! It was a great day when I was able to say "guaca-mole" a few months later. There were times of laughter and sweetness with seeing the children growing and moments of tears and grief.

During my hospital stay and the following months, my husband's response to the stroke and our life events served to show more about him and who he was and had always been. I could not cover for him anymore. Part of my reason I had been so driven to recover was that I was on my own even though we still lived in the same house. So, when the babies were ten months old, I found myself facing life as a divorced mother of three.

Far more devastating than a stroke, in a sense, is a painful divorce. I was humbled because although I had never verbalized it, I thought "that will never happen to me." Once again I had more grieving over the marriage that ended and what should have been. At the same time, I was encouraged by speech and cognitive progress. I did eventually relearn the alphabet and started by letter sounds to form words, sentences, and I can speak normally now. There are still deficits from the stroke but they are mostly unseen.

My children and I were able to move close to family. More than a decade later, we still feel the consequences of divorce; it is painful and complicated. And I have the opportunity to work through anger and bitterness...and every evening when the kids are cranky and needy and I'm tired and trying to cook dinner I am reminded once again that this is not the way it is supposed to be. But this is what it is, and I have been given the opportunity to ask God for help and see His provision and goodness in many ways.

Looking back at the time in my life that was busy and free from major suffer-ing, I'm grateful God gave me an opportunity to suffer..suffering has changed me and the changes God has brought about in me have been more valuable than just having an easy life.

For Reflection:

What stands out to you about Grace's story?

How does suffering increase the believer's ability to endure?

LIVING YOUR STORY

Leader Guidelines

SACRED STORY

Leader Guidelines

We are so excited you have decided to lead a group through this 10 week study!

You may be a seasoned leader and feel like you have a handle on the process; or you may be leading a group for the first time and feel like you are shaking in your boots. Either way, we want to offer resources as needed. Here are a few tips to help you make the most of your group time.

1. The ideal group size is 8-10 people including leader(s). Fewer is certainly okay! More than 10 may make it challenging for good discussion.

2. Consider leading the Bible study with a friend. One can host and the other can facilitate discussion, or you can take turns leading.

3. The study is designed ideally for an hour and a half discussion. If you are leading a morning or lunch-time group, it is possible to cover the material in an hour if time is short.

4. There are two options for your group. Either you can opt for the "no homework" approach which means that the time you spend together is used working through the questions as you go, looking up the verses and discussing each question. The other approach is for members to do the lesson ahead of time on their own and then spend the group time sharing what is learned. Either approach can work. Make the best decision based on your group's needs and background and what seems most comfortable.

5. Consider inviting women who you have regular contact with whether in your neighborhood, apartment complex, or work place. If you have a high school group or college friends you also see on a regular basis this is a great option as well.

6. Send out an email inviting them to your study. Keep it simple! Here is a sample.

   Subject line: "Does your story count?" or "How can you live your story?"

   "Hi Friends,

   Sally and I would like to invite you to my home for a ten-week Bible study called Living Your Story. *The study covers these relevant topics about what matters in living your story: Relationships, Freedom, Surrender, Obedience, Transformation, Identity, Contentment, Purpose, Forgiveness, and Endurance. It doesn't matter if you have never been in a Bible study. We would love for you to join. We will start in two weeks on _____ and meet from 7:30-9:00.*

   We will get back to you with more details. Have a good week!"

7. Plan on easy refreshments. Nothing too complicated!

8. Open and close with prayer. You and your co-leader can do this. As the study progresses you can ask if someone would like to volunteer to open or close.

9. Purpose Matters occurs toward the end of the series. The session encourages women to make a difference in the lives of others. Consider planning a gathering individually or together as a way to reach out to women who are not in the study. You may want to schedule the outreach to take place after the remaining sessions in the series are completed. Challenge the women in your study to launch studies of their own. Contact us at Sacred Story (contact@sacredstoryministries.org) to brainstorm outreach ideas.

10. Consider building in a time during the study for women in your group to share their stories each gathering. To keep the time consistent, ask a group member to set a timer (i.e. 7 minutes), allowing a woman to share whatever she'd like about her story within the time frame. You can ask women to volunteer or if the group agrees, draw names. Emphasize to the women that they do not need to prepare but instead share from their hearts.

11. Be sure to read through the story at the end and review the questions as a group. We have found women are encouraged by the stories which relate to the theme of the study.

12. Pray weekly for your group members. Pray that their eyes are open to the truth of the Gospel and that lives are changed.

13. We would love to see the faces of those doing your study and hear feedback! Please take a photo of your group at some point and email it along with your feedback on the material to contact@sacredstoryministries.org.

Thank you for launching a study. We are praying for you and anticipate the Lord doing great things in your group!

Sacred Story Ministries

Made in United States
Orlando, FL
19 September 2022

22584519R00041